ALTERNATIVE WICCA

The expansion of consciousness regards natural magick & its application in Contemporary Wiccan practises

KEITH MORGAN

FIRST EDITION YULE (December) 1991ev
FIRST REPRINT EOSTRA (March) 1994ev

ISBN NUMBER : 1 872189 46 6

PUBLISHED BY PENTACLE ENTERPRISES

Book Artwork by Elizabeth Taylor

A FULL CATALOGUE OF PENTACLE ENTERPRISES BOOKS &
ASSOCIATED PRODUCTS ARE AVAILABLE FROM THE ADDRESS
BELOW, FREE OF CHARGE. PLEASE MENTION THIS BOOK WHEN
ORDERING YOUR FREE CATALOGUE

THANK YOU FOR BUYING THIS BOOK
& SUPPORTING PENTACLE ENTERPRISES

PENTACLE ENTERPRISES
BM PENTACLE
LONDON WC1N 3XX

ALTERNATIVE WICCA

CONTENTS

ABOUT THE AUTHOR

Keith Morgan was born in Cheshire in 1961. He studied various Occult teachings from the age of 11 & was initiated into the craft of the wise in 1977.

He continues to work as a practising High priest of Wicca, & as a publisher & author in many esoteric fields. He writes in a simple & concise style which is easily understood by both the initiate & the student of the occult arts.

Keith is proud & outspoken about his beliefs, he has given interviews on local & national TV & radio & continues to be in the forefront of developing new ideas about all Occult teachings & paths.

Keith is also the editor of The Deosil Dance, the most radical of all Pagan & occult magazines around today

Anna Greenwood

INTRODUCTION.

The concept of this book is to expand peoples consciousness with regards to not only the magickal energies that surround us, but also to their concept of Wicca, or the Old religion, being that of the Pagan Pre-Christian Religious culture.

I intend to attempt to re-introduce to what is commonly called, the pagan/Wiccan or Occult orientated community, to the concept of Magick as a pure force within itself & in the differing ways it can be used, interpreted & applied, in a way, which I think has sadly been forgotten, & if it is not reminded about to a wider audience, then, as Wicca is developing, I feel we will lose the essential simplicity & with it the simple power that a natural understanding to a natural force like magick can bring.

Magick does not only exist within a circle, (a phrase you will be hearing often through this book, as a keyphrase to break the Cabbalistic orientated mystique of 'Circlework' as being tantamount to the common practise of 'Working Magick'). Magick is all around us, as it is as natural a force as any other natural manifestation of energy, such as naturally occurring electricity.

Because of what may be seen as content of this book, being of a contemporary nature is not a book suggested for the beginner, nor for anyone at an intermediatory state, the reason being is that any one at this stage will be enduring enough confusions, with so many other books, often contradicting themselves, I do not wish to add to this confusion, by my own revolutionary input into magickal practise. I would recommend that this book is the fourth in sequence & falls after THE HARMONICS OF WICCA, & feel that anybody who has taken the theology of HARMONICS ON BOARD, would be in a position to understand what is being put forward in this book.

I would not be decrying the point of this book, if I was to say that it was a manual of working for the Priest, priestess or Shaman of the Old Ways, rather than for the raw beginner, as by reaching these markers of achievement, different ways of working can be offered (on the whole), without instilling that all to destructive a force - confusion!

The contents of this book, its applications & suggestions need careful consideration, in how they apply to you & your own working potential in raising the energies of the Earth & relating them to the circumstances in which you choose to work through via magickal energies.

The instruction that this manual contains is not one of dogma, it is one of suggestion, & the main suggestion is that one should not knock it until one tries it, anything that may seem to be conflicting with ones already well held concepts, simply needs meditating upon, & reflecting upon in a manner that relates the concept to yourself.

As this book is not written for the beginner, some of the concepts that it contains could be seen to be revolutionary, again, I do not decry that this may be the case, but as this book has been written for what is a potential leadership within a group situation, it is an instructors manual.

I have felt a constant need for this type of suggestive writing, during the immediate past, as the one thing that the 1980's did show us, in a magickal sense, was a very much lack of direction with regards to a strong leadership, & instructive roleplay for group leaders (however loosely you wish to view a group, whether in an anarchistic sense, of all putting in input for the greater good, or in a strict coven sense, of hierarchy, both types of group essential, & both having very much of a lesson for each other), & accordingly, the values that such can give to a group situation.

I think that as a community, again on a very loose level, all interacting with each other, & as such having a responsibility to each other via that interaction, we have to be honest with ourselves, & admit, that what we have at the moment within pagan circles is not one of strong groups, with a strong leadership, being there, being available, & most of all being accountable for their actions & the actions of the groups that they are running.

What we have now, is for the greater part a lot of people running around like headless chickens, not admitting to themselves let alone any one else, that what they are doing is crap, they are talking crap, believing in crap & most criminal of all, passing crap on to gullible students who do not know better than to ask WHY!

The reason for this? EGO!

The ego of the individual on their own little power trips, as being one that will not admit when they do not know something, when they feel that they would be lacking, or worst of all, seen as lacking, by students, if they said I DO NOT KNOW!

Of course, to make a statement such as the last 2 paragraphs to be considered as a sweeping statement for the bulk of the Pagan community is again CRAP!

There are many excellent groups out there, many self educated Witches, pagans & shamans, all as valid as any coven initiated wise one, as they have learned the lessons of life, rather than having it given on a plate, as so many other people expect.

The path of attainment, of the point of development of knowing,

YES, I KNOW I AM A WISE ONE!, that is a difficult statement to make if one has not had guidance in the form of a role model within the Pagan/Occult community, again simply because of a lack of strong leadership.

The way of the wise one is a long path & a hard path to walk, true wise ones walk it & make a point of learning the lessons of that path, those that struggle really have to ask themselves, have I made it, & those that have had a light journey, have to ask themselves, have I really made it! was it really that easy?

I think that can assess the whole point of this book, the ability to make a third party consider magickal pondering's in a relative application to themselves, to their own magick & to the interaction of that magick in their everyday life.

Unlike television, being chewing gum for the eyes, I would take it that this book is laxative for the head! (it removes crap!)
     In the recent past, I have been accused by at least one person to my face & several others behind my back, that I was anti establishment, anarchistic & in possession of a self centred ego, simply because of what I write about flies in the face of what most people would see as being 'Mainstream Wicca'.

3

This attitude I find pathetic, as the critics who knock what I am trying to get over to a wider audience have not even met me, or discussed any opinions that I have with me. One of the largest back handed compliments that have been given me, was to define my path as being of 'Sh'ite Wicca!' (pagan fundamentalist maybe!!!!), I would prefer to define myself as being of a Progressive Modernistic Wiccan belief, in that I believe that Wicca is not only an ancient belief, & that what goes in circles, will eventually come to the fore.

The beliefs of our ancestors are valid, as valid as an established religion as any other, but we are not living in a time warp, for those philosophies to be valid, we have to be able to relate to them today & they have to make sense in our chartering of our ship of life through the rough seas of living! We need a sturdy boat to travel in & that boat is our faith in the Old ones!

Within this book, I am not imposing my will or views upon others, I am merely suggesting alternative attitudes that we can encounter upon our Magickal path, & if possible, to sow the seed of self determination within our students to seek further for enlightenment rather than from the 'occult sector' of the new Age community..

It is a re-dressing of true ancient ways of working that have brought the Old Religions & faiths away from the Quasi/Masonic/Cabbalistic ways of working that have crept into Wicca since it came out of the closet. Some home truths have to be tackled head on, & this is what I hope to do not out of Bitchcraft, but in an attempt to be honest in re asserting ancient tribal ways of working into Wicca.

Magick is not confined to the realms of the Magickal circle, it is to be found in many aspects throughout nature, & why not, after all what is Magick if not a natural force. Magick is the co relationship of harnessing or manipulation & harmonious working with, elemental forces of nature.

Magick is not a supernatural concept but one that is entirely natural & harmonious with our pagan reverence of the Earth & its spirit, as a Goddess & a God - our ancient deities.

We will also be focusing upon the differing concepts of ritual, their importance & their overuse, so we can assess what our needs are today & in which way we can use the ritual & ceremonial technique to the best of our effects.

We will be looking at the many ways in which we can use different techniques from many different pagan tribal situations worldwide, all of which we can use ourselves today.

But most of all, we will be looking at the ways in which we can relate to what we can only assume to be alternative magick, alternative that is until we adopt it!

THE PURPOSE OF RITUAL

Parts of this chapter in underlined Italics, are quotations from THE HARMONICS OF WICCA, & have been included & expanded upon, to give definition between Ritual & ceremony, for further detail of this consult THE HARMONICS OF WICCA.

The need to distinguish between ritual & Ceremony is great, & many people are confusing the two, thus alienating the purpose of both ritual & ceremony. In Harmonics of Wicca, I gave a definition of ritual being

""*A spiritually enlightening act or series of acts, that have many uses within the magickal development of a person.*""

Ritual is important to a person & to their development in a magickal manner, it is a milestone along a path & lets face it, we need milestones in all walks of life, to indicate how far we have gone & how far we need to go. On a spiritual path where the goal is never in sight, & where the path has no end, this can be confusing, however, our milestones are conscious realisations of achievements & the confidence we have in those achievements, that we are capable of being able to perform these acts that we have learned, without ant fear as to our inability to be able to do them in a responsible manner.

""*Ritual can enhance any magick being performed, by attuning the subconscious into a frame of mind in which the natural Magickal energies are easier to put into action, whilst performing the Magick.*""

Any act done in a 'Ritual' manner, enhances the magickal objective of the act, take for example a Tarot reader, we will call her Selene, about to do a reading for a person, she follows a set pattern of actions that she has always done to attune herself to the situation & the person. She will first greet the person & escort her to her table, she will ask the person her name, whilst she is unwrapping her tarot, that she normally keeps in a box, on a special table, that contains a Candle, Incense burner, & statues of the Lord & lady of the Old Religion.

Whilst she is shuffling her own tarot cards she is talking to her client, who she then asks to take hold of her cards & shuffle them until she feels happy about it. Selene then lays the cards out upon a special cloth that her cards were wrapped in. She then performs the reading for the client, at the end of the reading she asks her client if she is happy with the reading & has she any questions. If there is she answers them. She then wraps her cards up, places them back inside the box & on the special table with her other accoutrements. The client then pays Selene & leaves.

The question is, was that ritual or was that ceremony?

Let us analyse what has gone on;

" She will first greet the person & escort her to her table."
 Selene is making this client feel at ease within what could be a strange situation, the client knows that she is there for something out of the ordinary to take place, Selenes greeting allays her fear & starts to break down any barriers the client may have.

"She will ask the person her name, whilst she is unwrapping her tarot, that she normally keeps in a box, on a special table, that contains a Candle, Incense burner, & statues of the Lord & lady of the Old Religion."
 By asking the client her name, she is building up a rapport with this person & starting to get to know her on different levels. When Selene produces her cards from her altar, the client is obviously impressed, as she is confronted with items she may not encounter in everyday life, namely, tarot, incense, candles, & other esoterica. This has a shattering effect on her subconsciously, & all of a sudden , any jest as to the validity of the reading goes, as she is confronted with a person performing a set of moves, which she, the client deems to be some significant ritual done for here benefit.

"Whilst she is shuffling her own tarot cards she is talking to her client, who she then asks to take hold of her cards & shuffle them until she feels happy about it."
 The shuffling of the cards is again more ritualistic moves to impress the seriousness of the situation onto the client. The clients shuffling impressed the clients own Karma upon the cards.

"Selene then lays the cards out upon a special cloth that her cards were wrapped in. She then performs the reading for the client, at the end of the reading she asks her client if she is happy with the reading & has she any questions. If there is she answers them."

More ritualistic moves impressing seriousness, thus is the reading taken seriously, any questions are answered by the reader, thus taking upon herself the role of teacher & spiritual guide.

"She then wraps her cards up, places them back inside the box & on the special table with her other accoutrements."

Ritualistic moves that impress the importance of the cards among their presence of other holy objects upon her altar, remember, this is probably the clients first taste & experience of a magickal act, so it will all seem mysterious if not spooky!

"The client then pays Selene & leaves."

This is important for the client, by paying on a financial level, she is forced to take seriously the reading that has gone beforehand, if she is not required to pay at least something, relating to her financial situation, she will not take seriously what has gone before, & regard it as parlour games or fortune telling.

After analysis, was that ritual or ceremony?

The fact is, it was ceremony, it was a ceremonial act of magick, designed to give another person guidance upon many levels of consciousness.

Take another example, again using the concept of Selene, as the archetypical wise one. Her friend Helen, has asked Selene to perform a spell to aid her in passing her driving test. Helen knows about Selenes involvement with things magickal, & trusts her to perform the act.

Selene instructs Helen to bathe, dress in a white robe & join her in her temple. When Helen enters the temple, Selene is already bathed & in her ritual robes, a circle is cast around the two, & Incense is liberally used, as is anointing oils etc.

After the casting of the circle, Prayers are offered to the mighty ones of the universe, the Lord & lady, the powers of the elements.

In Front of Helen the spell is cast, & empowered, using a candle, cord, more incense & magickal tools. Helen is told that for the spell to work, she must offer to the Old ones a sacrifice, thus paying for what she has received. her sacrifice, is that she will spend 100 hours picking litter up from a heavily littered woodland. Helen accepts this & a bargain is struck.

The circle is banished & the pair retire from the temple, none of this is spoke of again by either of them

Again, is this Ritual or Ceremony?
   Several correlating facts are seen between the spell & the Tarot reading, except with the spell a greater intensity of force was needed & obtained, the payment for the spell, was also greater on Helens part,. 100 hours of picking up rubbish, could also be seen as being a magickal act, as all the while that she would be picking it up, she would be remembering the reason that she was doing this for.

Selene has been recognised as being a wise one, by virtue of the wisdom that she exudes in her contact with other people, therefore she has been trusted by Helen, to be responsible enough to perform what is a vital ritual for her.

In both circumstances,
1; A person Has come for help from a third party
2; Help was freely given
3; Certain ritualised movements were performed
4; Payment was required in both instances.

   The above was in fact a ritual not a ceremony The thing that distinguished it from a ceremony, is the fact that Selene, in performing her drawing & summoning of energy via the circle, was performing a ritual where as the ceremony of the Tarot reading did not have as much of the energy involved as the ritual did.

   It may be seen as being pedantic about drawing correlations between ritual & ceremony, but it is important, rituals are rites of passages & as such should only need to be performed once for a particular person,Baptism (Wiccaning), Initiation, Ordination, Handfasting, Requiem. Helens driving test could also be seen as being a rite of passage, in that it is a ritual that only needs to be done once.

Ceremony however, is something that can be done time & time again, all with differing consequences, ceremony can include, sweat Lodges, Celebration of seasonal turnings(Sabbats), Tarot readings, healing etc, all can be done within the confines of a ceremony, rather than a ritual. Ritual has a strange effect upon a group of people, it can be a bonding, an establishing of a communal or clan tie, ceremony.

"If there is more than one person performing the rite then it can have a unifying effect upon the group, within the people individually involved & with the natural elemental forces. It can be a knowledgeable experience for the people involved, gaining direct knowledge from each other & from the elements invoked within the ritual. But most of all;- IT IS A TOTALLY SPIRITUAL EXPERIENCE IN WHICH THE PARTICIPANTS MEET THEIR SPIRITUAL GUIDES/ EXPRESSIONS OF THE DEITIES THEY ARE IN CONTACT WITH.

This could well occur within ceremony, but is more than likely to occur within ritual, as the energies raised within ritual is far stronger, & to be quite honest, is far more demanding upon the people involved, Ritual should never be taken lightly, the circle, is a place between the worlds of Man & spirit, & too many people fail to realise that when they wish to start performing ' Rituals'.

Our ancestors of times past did not use the merest of excuses to perform rituals, to them, rituals were rites of passage, ceremonies however were commonplace & frequent, at the special times of the Year, the Sabbats, people would gather, to make merry & to 'party' if we can view it that way, in celebration of the Old Gods & Goddesses not to mark the passing of the year in a ritualistic sense.

"If people could live more in harmony with the earth today, they would find little reason in celebrating Natural cycles of the earth in a ritual context (more often than not in an indoor 'Temple' situation) when they would be partaking in a permanent ritual of living within the cycles of the Earth. THE TRUE RITE OF PASSAGE OF MAN!.

At the Sabbats people could once again meet up with like minded folk, as the did of Old, to praise the Old Gods, in celebration. This occurred in times past,& gives the accounts in History of the Great Sabbats where hundred of witches would attend feasting & making merry.

If this was done, & the amount of 'Play' rites were lessened, then the few rituals that todays Pagans were performing would have far greater relevance for them throughout their lives, & would truly mark changing points & highlights within their lives.

Ceremony should replace Ritual on the greater part to give far more respect to ritual in people: lives & to truly give ritual an aspect of marking the changing phases of their lives. We follow set patterns of ceremonies every day, ritual is something else, that takes on a far greater aspect within our lives, & as such gives deeper meaning to a symbolic rite rather than a ceremonial act.

ALTERNATIVE RITUAL
& CEREMONIAL TECHNIQUE

The standard Circle within Wiccan & other Pagan working groups, usually consists of the following scenario;

Consecration of water & salt

Invocation of the elements

Casting of the Circle

Invocation of the deities

Consecration of the Cakes & Ale

Any magickal working

Banishing of the circle

The greater part of this set ritual format, is essentially based upon earlier Cabbalistic rites, as in those practised by the Golden Dawn, & other Cabbalistic groups at the beginning of this century, & which have a pedigree of possible no more than 200 years previous.

They were included within Wiccan rituals, by writers of such rituals, or should I say for rituals ascribing to belong to the Wiccan tradition, for no other reason other than that was the established format for 'Occult orientated ritual', & rather than seeing to be differing from the norm, borrowed heavily upon the established writings etc which were available, which by todays standards were minimal.

As the set up, is of another tradition, the smaller composite ceremonies, making up the larger scenario of ritual, is seen within the ritual as being more of a filling in process, where it is seen to be something to do rather than the raising of energy, which surely is the essential purpose of the ritual (oh no! look at all the hard line dyed in the wool Saturday night Knifewavers coming for my blood!....hang on kids, wait for a freak out until the end of chapter, all will be revealed!).

If we break down this kind of ritual, & look at the individual aspects of what comprises of a 'standard Wiccan/Pagan circle', we can see that as a ritual, It is far far removed from the rituals of our ancestors, whilst we do not know exactly what they did do, WE KNOW WHAT THEY DID NOT DO, & that is follow a tradition of a Judaic culture, whilst in these islands, & manifest it as the indigenous Pagan religious activity of these lands. Indigenation really is something of an anathema, as the blessed isles of Albion, did not every have a 'Race of people'. of its own, but has always been a melting pot of colours, tribes,, races etc, yes even our neolithic ancestors hiked it over from the continent!

Because of this melting pot of tribes & traditions, we have a composite view of what our Pagan ancestors assimilated as their religious practise, but as Judaism was not even around at this time, it is hardly likely that any Cabbalistic correspondences are prominent!

Anyway, back to the analysis, of what is seen as Wiccan ritual.

Consecration of water & salt - The blessing of the elements prior to using them within the circle. A very valid part of the ritual as being a blessing for purity, something which has always been foremost even in the most ancient of ritual, in that a purity in all things is utmost

Invocation of the elements- The summoning of the powers of the Elements to be present within the ritual, The Invocation of elemental energies.

Casting of the Circle- The drawing together of all the energies raised within the circle, as well as unifying the people involved within the ritual. The circle, is a place between the worlds of man & spirit, but also, is a place where all are equal, whether they be human or element. All have a place within the circle, & it is the circle that pulls them together. The invocation of the unity of the elemental energies, each being bound with each other.

Invocation of the deities- The act of devotion to the particular deities that one is working with, recognising that individual deities are personalised manifestations of the Lord & Lady. The invocation of the energies of the deities, manifesting themselves through the energies of the elements, as each of the elements are respective manifestations of both Male & female aspects of divinity,

So it is that the male & female aspects of divinity are also composite of the 4 base elements, creating the fifth ethereal element of spirit, it is the Animus within the Anima once again.

Consecration of the Cakes & Ale- The blessing & acknowledgement of good things to eat & drink, as being gifts of the Lord & the Lady. Association with Eucharistic communion aspects is not acknowledged, as within this ceremony, it is not the transmutation of the Bread or wine into any particular manifestation of deity, leading to ritualistic cannibalism upon ingestion (as in later religions!), but the devout & sincere thanks for the gifts of the Gods, as being food for the ingestion of all living creatures, including mankind. The eucharistic transmutation does not occur by magickal means, as in Christian High Mass, simply because the element of divinity is already present within the food, & does not need the Priest to invoke the power within the food, as Food, is part of the Earth, so it is contains the 5 elements again, & once again, by becoming part of us (you are what you eat!), so we are one with those elements, & those elements are one with us, but also, as those elements are one with divinity (being God & Goddess), then we are one with the God & Goddess, via the spiritual associations of the food that we ingest, this is recognised within ritual, & so we have the consecration & acknowledgement of the Cakes & Ale as being manifestations via the composite elements as being gifts from the Gods.,

Any magickal working - Often the whole purpose of the ritual, is a small piece of magickal working, a spell perhaps, lasting no more than 10 minutes, or a prayer of devotion , was all the above really necessary for this one small act of magickal energy direction?

Banishing of the Circle- The closing down of a circle as being finished & of no more use within this particular circumstance.

As well as the above, upon 'Sabbats' & 'Esbats', it may be the purpose for the ritual, so prayers associated with that occasion will be spoken, often read from a book, often the words of someone else repeated parrot fashion as will most of the above!

What I want to put forward, is that it is well documented among many sources, that the Practice of the Old Ways, the beliefs of our Pagan ancestors, includes Dancing, chanting, rhythmic drumming or beating, ecstatic expressive shouting, the use of what we may describe as drugs, which in effect are but natural substances, plants etc. etc.

Gerald B Gardner, in his books on Witchcraft described the dances of the Witches of the Middle ages, as being something between a volita & a foxtrot, in other words, as an energetic & frivolous, joyous dance step, probably a remnant from the days of orgiastic & frenzied dance. I suppose if one was doing the same anthropological study about todays tribal situation, one could describe the frenzied dance leading to exstasis as being the Jive, the headbang or the Pogo!

Of late, the concept of ritual within Wicca that most Wiccans adopt, is of more of a Cabbalistic orientation of declarations of words, & symbolic gestures, rather than a ritual that should come from the heart, & emotions, rather than from the writings of another person repeated ad verbatim, from the 'Sacred Book of shadows - often a loose leaf folder from W H Smiths, written in best Sunday handwriting, forgetting the ancient formula for magickal ink, sacred ballpoint pens, duly consecrated for the job suffice!).

If ritualistic Wicca today, was a direct descendant from the pre Christian ritual magick of our ancestors, then, as our ancestors rituals were all different from each others, as per the rituals of one tribe were not the rites of another tribe. Then, today, we would have the concept of different covens using vastly different rituals, sadly however, upon the whole we do not, simply because a set of Dogmatic principles & the concept of the CORRECT WAYS OF WORKING are being rammed down peoples throats & the cloning system is well under way to turn everyone's into a set pattern that is familiar to all.

What we do have is the ritualistic aspects of Wicca descending not from our Pagan ancestors, but from a Middle age concept of Judeo-Christian mysticism, & its later descendants of Golden dawn, orientation of ritual, as in   Casting a   circle, Lord of the watchtowers etc.

In fact much ritual that is enacted today within many Covens all over the world, have no greater ancestral lineage than from Janet & Stewart Farrars book 'Eight Sabbats for witches', not that I am putting the book down far from it, it is an excellent example of a collection of seasonal & other rituals, that Janet & Stewart gladly admit is their own creation, & who recommend that people adapt, recreate & use within their own frameworks etc, rather than what is occurring, & that is the ad verbatim, parrot fashion repetition of their words.

Despite the US version being called 'The Witches Bible Vol. 1', I hardly think it was Janet & Stewarts intention to compile a holy book for use on a parity with the Q'uran, the Torah or the New testament, could we see the day however, where Wiccans would choose to swear an oath on the Book of Shadows - or the Witches Bible Vol. 1 ?

One reason for the non committal of Wiccans to experiment could be that they are unfamiliar with the true essence of natural power, & the fact that such power extends from themselves, & by using another persons magickal words then that will somehow be more powerful than their own heartfelt emotions, which of course they will not.

I must stress at this point, (& why this book was not recommended for beginners) that for all beginners or for people very inexperienced within the Magickal arts & what is expected of them, & what they should be comfortable with & what they should be sure of. To a beginner, experience can only come with the security with working with something that they have the utmost of security with & that is usually the written word of their Priest/ess, Teacher or guide.

It must be stressed however that that eventual goal will be to wean the neophyte off the written word & for them to create rituals that come from within rather than without, & for them to have the confidence within themselves to understand & appreciate the magick that comes from within their own words, & that such a magick will be far more potent than the second hand emotions of another person.

From this conglomeration of traditions of many paths, what we do have today, is some (not all!) covens working in a very dogmatic & non constructive way, of a critical attitude towards other peoples rituals occurring, especially if that person is doing something unfamiliar to the resident critic, criticism through unfamiliarity & the suspicion that it arouses is very negative.

It is this Negativity borne out out of unfounded criticisms of that which may seem strange to the uninitiated of that group etc that is creating the false division within 20th century pagan circles. We are responsible for killing off our own future, by creating disunity today within groups who may not be of our own choosing - but is that our right to say so? No, each is allowed their own license to ritually work in whatever way they choose, what they are not allowed to do, by the very laws of decency that we, as Humans should live by, is to either lie, bullshit or create a false mythos around them or their group this giving an air of respectability to something that is far from it, by rubbishing out other people, other magickal traditions, or especially, other people performing those rites.

As a brief diversity (shall we call it a 'brief commercial break in the big feature' for a little culture!) on the subject of 'Morality & respectability' within our behaviour in the way we interact with our peer group, I choose to take my guidelines from nature, & as in the Book The Wicker Man by Anthony Schaeffer & to listen to what Lord Summerisle has to say on this matter;

"I think I could turn & live with animals, they are so placid & self contained, they do not lie awake in the dark & weep for their sins, they do not make me sick discussing their duty to God, not one of them kneels to another, or to his own kind that lived thousands of years ago. Not one of them is respectable, or unhappy all over the Earth!"

It has been suggested to me, though not directly to my face, that because, I have used black candles within a circle, that I work very much within the realm of the underworld & can equate with the deities of such, & what may be considered dark deities, Morrigan, Janus etc & because I have cast a circle widdershins within a burial chamber that I am a black magician!

This mentality is absurd, & is divisive & sectionary within Wicca & Paganism of all persuasions. Them morality of questioning my actions is something not unlike Lord Summerisle's questioning of other religious beliefs, yet he does it out of knowledge, he rejects

17

that which is not relevant to his own philosophies out of knowledge of that path, how can someone know where my moralities lie, within a ritual in burial chamber, if they have yet to walk the path I tread.

Is there something to be feared in the underworld that I am home in ?

Is there some suspicion as to why I cast a circle widdershins on a plane of consciousness that is a reversal to this positive Earth planes, do two positives not make a negative & two negatives a positive.

As for black candles - As colour as we know is is differing frequencies of light (diffracted for visual experience by a spectrum), observed by the very presence of light, then in a world where there is no light, what colour is the colour of a world devoid of all colour, where light is minimal ? Black!

I must stress, that I do agree that to a beginner, or to a person who is not yet understanding of the natural elemental laws of magick, that a circle should be cast within a Deosil direction, as being in the way of the sun, this way, any effects the circle has, will be of a generating effects remotely different from a widdershins circle, which may be cast, to impact the effects of the ritual upon the group.

Much in the same way, that workings within a burial chamber, may not be seen as necromancy, for lest we forget, that elaborate burial chambers, like Barclodiadd Y gawrs & Bryn Celli Ddu on Anglesey, Newgrange in Ireland, & Wayland Smithy in the South of England, are not only places of disposal of human remains, but are sacred temples constructed within the Earth Mother, as a womb of the Earth mother, in which it is possible to work magick, by our being within the wombs, we magickal sperm of the Lord & lady returning to our womb to become one with the cosmic egg of creation, we are getting back to our magickal roots by becoming one with the magickal essence of a magickal place that was & will always be, held sacred to our ancestors.

The most impressive feeling one gets from burial chambers is that they are also initiatory chambers, where a confrontation occurs, between the worlds of man & spirit, between the dead & the living, & between the Goddess, whose womb is the chamber, & the Horned God, whose spirit of the dead is all present!

We must look towards techniques of what we, may consider to be associate cultures, & not repeat them parrot fashion, but harness the technique & potential of associate cultures, & merge them within our own.

What I am saying, is if it don't fit, Don't force it!

This is what has happened in the past, we have had Cabbalistic, Gnostic Christianity, Islamic & Masonic influences crop up within Wicca, & as such has weakened the essential spirit of Wicca. There are some things which do not fit, have never fitted & are seen today as being of a totally alien religious & social culture & will not fit no matter how enthusiastic the call for a fit is!

These alien concepts are usually consisting of a selection of the following;-

The concept of any religious God image from any non pagan culture as a cross infection of pagan deity. This includes the Christ figure as a pagan 'Sun God'; The Image of the Virgin Mary as a Goddess, Jehovah as a Horned God etc etc The same can be said for Mohammed, Buddha, Fatima, Moses, Abraham, Noah etc etc. A Pagan deity precedes all other deities & should always be recognised as so. Pagan beliefs were nearly wiped our by Christian infiltration in the Dark Ages, when the confidence tricksters that were Christian missionaries tried to pull the above stunts in an effort to undermine the importance of the Pagan deities & the easy installation of the Newer man made Deities.

The totemic use of animals that are not indigenous to a land that is unfamiliar with these totemic images, Including the 'Thunderbird' or 'coyote', within rituals in the lands of where I am writing this for (the Lands of Albion though I do concede that this book will also be read in the USA, where these animals will be relevant to ritual), like many other animals that are alien to the spirit of these lands, if we are alien to these animals, we cannot equate with them on a spiritual/magickal level.

The invocation of the Goddess Isis, or the God Osiris, as via Egyptian symbology, as manifestations of the Lord & Lady of Wicca, again in these lands. The same is said for other deity names, from other cultures that are alien to the lands in which they are invoked.

The invocation of the ancestral spirit of Australasia Aborigine Amerind Ancestors - as though they who have walked this land.

None of this fits our natural concept of a magickal environment, simply because it is alien not only to the lands in which we inhabit, but also to ourselves & our genetic make-up, our link with our ancestry which we carry with us, & which we will pass down to our children.

As we are our ancestors, so will be part of our own future as we will be passing down our genetic codes via our DNA & with it, we will be passing on our influences to later generations.

What could be seen to fit, within the magickal realms of the lands in which we inhabit as well as the bodies that we inhabit & the codes that we pass down to future generations, must be concepts that are harmonious with our initial philosophies & these are concepts such as;

The association of the Amerind Medicine Wheels - once correctly aligned to our Wiccan concept of elemental/directional association, which is needed, to be compatible with our own ways of working that are harmonious with the spirit of the lands in which we are working (see the Harmonics of Wicca for details of this re alignment).

The use of frenzied dance, & drumming - as in the concept of afro/Caribbean induced Voudoun worship, this is one of the ways how our ancestors raised energy, & how all ancestors raised energy in all traditions worldwide.

The use of Totemic animals, that are indigenous to the lands in which one is working in - Thunderbird, bears, & coyotes are fine within the American continent, but much more preferable to use Owls, Wildcats, & foxes of these lands. Not only are they far more easy to associate with, but as most people have not even seen a bear or a coyote or a condor, close to hand, how can they relate with the essential spirit of such an animal. One cannot relate to that which one has not seen or experienced!.

The use of art within ritual - as in Navaho sand painting, Tibetan thangkas, Indian Mandala's. Not forgetting of course our own heritage of Celtic, Pictish Saxon & Nordic artworks - We can use the many techniques of all indigenous people, combine them with the symbology of our own cultures to create our own spiritual artistic technique that will link our sub conscious into the greater consciousness of the Earth.

I am sure that I can offer the idea to you for you to work on in your own style of how to create alternative ritual & ceremony that we can use to tap into the greater spiritual development that is Wicca & paganism within the New Age

When creating alternative ritual using a combination of ceremonial & ritual technique from many 'Pagan' cultures, please be sure to make allowances for the following considerations to be a priority within your workings.

Ceremonies & rituals

1; That energy is raised within ceremonies & rituals be done so positively for positive reasons. the definition between ceremony & ritual must be respected

2; That the invocation of elements is complete within such rituals, no element is left out, nor any one element is enforced more than another. The same also goes for the emphasis upon the duality of Male & female, Wicca is a dualistic approach & as such we have to accept the importance of both the masculine & feminine, that is within us all, we have to accept this & realise that both the Male & female aspects need to be represented within our rituals & that a balance be maintained at all times, that way a bias will not be evident & with it imbalance.

3; That the devotion of the ritual or ceremony be directed towards Pagan deities of corresponding Pagan cultures, (No Invocation to Odin & Isis in the same rites!) that one is working with within the ritual.

4; That the force of the ritual be defined & directed towards the aim intended - no psychic vampires sapping off what they want is there?

5: That the ceremony performed is for the satisfaction of those involved, no room for error or doubt, thus negating the effect.

6: That it be culturally strong in its enactment or performance, that the energy directed is of equal importance to the energy received.

7: That the aspects of the ritual be appreciated by all concerned as being a serious magickal & religious experience, not just an act or 'something else' to do!. There are far too many failed actors & actresses getting off on the ritual aspects of Wicca, we do not need any more. Good acting may seem effective, but if it is shallow & without meaning then it is as valid as the next impotent religion!

It should also be remembered that a ritual is there for everyone gathered to be participating in, there should be no viewing without participation, as this is of a negative action to the end results of the ritual, this should be noted, too many people consider ritual & ceremony to be reminiscent of a voyeuristic peep show, especially with the emergence of organised media rituals, by a new breed of pagan known as media witches, who, to obtain credence for their ego, will organise a ritual solely for the media, & perform that ritual in such a choreographed manner, that it takes away any minuscule religious significance that it may once have held for them.

In 'media-rites' the ego of the attention seeking media hawks (People masquerading as devotional Wiccans to gain a certain amount of credibility on the backs of sincere people), has replaced the intention of the rite & its been replaced by the sole intention of the promotion of the ego for the media witch! .

WICCA & SHAMANISM

Within members of the Wiccan community, there is a certain amount of confusion, as to the inter relationship between Wicca & shamanism, are they compatible, or are they alien to each other.

They are of course one & the same thing, & that Wiccan & other Pagan beliefs are in effect the Shamanism, of the British Isles. To define this even further, I would have to correct this definition & say, that Wicca is the resurrected manifestation of modern Pagan practise, based upon ancient pagan beliefs, in that the way in which we perform ritual today, is most certainly not the way in which our ancestors performed their rituals, the method of working may have changed, but believe me the purposes are exactly the same;.

A lot of confusion has come from among newer members of the community, who are unsure as to the definition of title, something that we should be getting away from, because of the confusion caused by contradicting titles.

As with the entirety of this book, what follows then, are my theories regards the Archetypical roles of both Shaman & Witch, using the guidelines set out by what is expected of using the titles of Witch & Shaman.

As I have always maintained with all of my writings, I am not saying whether other peoples opinions or my own opinions are right or wrong, but what I am saying is that within this sphere of pagan philosophy, there is a differing of opinions as to title typecasting & it is for the reader to decide.

The Role of Shaman/Witch- The Role of a wise one.

When exploring the religious heritage of an indigenous people, there will be terminology used which may conflict when comparing differing traditions or tribes. Words are only used when describing something to a third party & the words Shaman & Witch have both been used over & over again in differing analogies - what are the meanings of these words.

WHAT IS A SHAMAN ?

A Shaman is the wise one of a tribal people, they were the ones who were held in great esteem as guardians of spiritual knowledge & mediators between the world of Man & spirit.

WHAT IS A WITCH ?

The word 'Witch' has been used to identify a wise one of the ancient religion of Wicca, the village wise one, the person who had a knowledge of the use of herbs, spells, potions, magick! They were also the person who understood the forces of nature & the magickal current within.

The Witch or wise one of the middle age village, was held in as much reverence as her tribal ancestor the Shaman from the millennia before. The witch of the village transcended from her tribal ancestral wise one, of whose job she was doing to the same efficacy.

If the wise one of the ancient tribes could be classed as a shaman, then why not our concept of the middle age witch - after all they were performing the same functions; that of spiritual mediator within their extended family that was either tribe or latterly village. The Role of shaman & witch were the same to our ancestors, it was merely a matter of time that divided both functions, the people were the same following the same roles expected of their status, as mediators between the seen & unseen.

Today, as the divide between cultures is at its greatest, it is the patriarchal stagnation of the late Piscean age that is bringing this about; through division of the people there is rule. People today are searching for greater validity to their lives, & as such are looking towards new age philosophies in a need for fulfilment.

People are once again turning towards the Pagan beliefs of their ancestors, as a need for spiritual fulfilment, including both Wicca other Pagan paths, & North American Shamanism.

Wicca & other pagan paths have a validation of their own as to the attunement of the concept & method of working within the British Isles, & in the lands of the Celts, Saxons, etc (in other words, the peoples of the paths which are Wiccan or Nordic etc), whilst North American Shamanism, has an eco-Global relationship with the spirit of the land of its ancestral inhabitants, the magickal energies raised by such ancestral linking via genetic composition.

With the emergence of the New Age Spirit, which has somewhat heralded a mass searching for pagan paths back to the God Head, people have been what one can only call 'Cobbling together' of paths & symbolism of those paths in creating what was the scourge of 20th century occultism, & that is generalised spirituality, where it did not matter that paths were incompatible or unassociated, if it eased a persons guilt of accusation of 'Dabbling in the Occult', then they would combine these incompatible ways to create a way that was 'safe' for them to follow, bogey men, nowhere to be seen!

Part of this New Age movement, creeping into ancient beliefs, included turning towards the concept of North American shamanism, as a need for spiritual fulfilment, but what people sadly fail to see is that in these lands, we have our own ancient spiritual path, complete with our own spirit world, deities, otherworld, totemic animals & teacher plants, all this is commonplace within Wicca- the old religion of these lands.

As Wicca was the buzz word of the 60's & 70's so is shamanism of the 80's & 90's, but are they so different ? The answer is no, for it is the context in which something is accepted rather than imposed upon that is important.

One of the assumptions that people, who have followed an established Pagan path, come to is that Worship of the Goddess & God archetypes is no longer sufficient, Wiccans are now experimenting in ritual, questioning the old tried & tested methods of working & indeed seeking a more personal form of enlightenment"

I think this has always been the case within Wicca, Native American Shamans, view the concept of Wakan tanka - the Great Spirit, as being Male & Female, exactly the same as Wiccans. Regards ritual, I think most progressive Wiccans & pagans view the concept of rituals, as being of a personal composition, rather than emulating the words of other peoples rituals, that are in books such as the Farrars, Valiente etc. The more personal enlightenment that occurs is the natural energy that Must be felt when one is in contact with the God & Goddess (Or Wakan Tanka if you so desire....what is the difference?)

Many of my own critics have been known to have stated something in the region of what follows (as being just one persons opinion)

" It has been suggested that Wicca & Shamanism are the same, this is of course, in my opinion ridiculous! Whilst Shamanism can happily coexist alongside another religion or religious beliefs it is not a religion "

This is so wrong & to state such is to say that our ancient pagan ancestors were an un religious society, this is the wrong information that fundamental religions give to discredit our Pagan beliefs by saying they are not of a religious nature.

Our ancestors were probably infinitely more religious than what many Pagans are today, as they live their beliefs daily rather than at certain times of the year! What has differed is the modernistic view of Wicca, in that it has been denigrated into the form of an extension of a hobby, rather than as a serious commitment to a lifetimes devotion, service & religious path, that has to be taken seriously, & one that needs as much commitment as any other religious path.

One cannot say that one is a Buddhist Witch, any more than one can say they are a white witch, or a black witch, or a Christian witch!

If a witch is a wise one, then it is a wise one of a Pagan way, it is complete within itself, & needs no reliance upon outside influences to make it appear credible, if more people were proud to define that they are PAGAN & PROUD, or GLAD TO BE A WICCAN!, then perhaps the credibility that our pagan ways deserve, would be given some respect from those of other religious paths, who would be then forced to sit down & talk with us, rather than be content with rubbishing our beliefs out because they consider them to be a threat to their own establishment!

Whether you view the forces of magick as being such or consider them to be 'Medicine',& lets face it, the concept of medicine being magick, is something which is indicative of creating good or well being) either way it is unimportant, it is the workings that matter, & the spiritual content of such. The ways of worship of our Celtic & Saxon ancestors were complete within themselves, they had no need to import any exterior concepts such as the worship of

Isis, they knew the correlation, & knew of all Gods being of the Force masculine, & respective with Feminine aspects of all Goddesses, but they also knew that the names used by their tribe, etc were personal to them & worked because they have always been used by them! Why import something from elsewhere when an old way sufficed needs for millennia!

People may feel a deep kinship with many other cultures from all aspects of Pagan or tribal knowledge, & may feel equally happy to work with one of the 'key elements ' supplied by their respective tradition,   in exactly the same way that I can also work quite happily with 'Keys' of all cultures, working within that culture & Geography. (& the alternativeness of which I hope I am managing to express in this book)

I know of no Celtic Wiccan/Shaman that would easily invoke Isis within these lands, when we have more than enough archetypes of the Great Mother in her many manifestations, Arianrhod, Rhiannon, Ceredwenn etc etc If I was doing a ritual in Egypt, I would happily work with the essential spirit that is Isis, in that Land, in the same way that if I was worshipping the Goddess in Nordic lands, I would attune to her via Freya.

Differences between Shamans & Wiccans could be said to exist in the way that (& I Quote)

". A shamans main objective is to establish otherworld contact   using   a   myriad of 'keys', including; Music, Dance, fasting, Drugs, Totem animals etc. The Shamanic role therefore is as an intermediary. "

I have to ask that is this also not what our Pagan ancestors & those of us following a Pagan way in these blessed isles have always done, they contacted the astral worlds, via the use of herbs, natural drugs (Incenses etc), Music dance etc, it is only of latter years as Wicca has become highly ritualised, formalised & associated with 'The Occult' Cabbala, & other esotericism, that people were moving away from these natural ways of working. - thankfully today people are once again moving back to the old ways (in a real sense) by adopting the old ways of workings, rather than ritual for ritual sake!

We of a Traditional Craft consider ourselves to be representatives of the Spirit plane manifested upon the Earth Plane, we are Otherworld contacts, working with the elements of this world & using the spirit energy of the Underworld/Otherworld in exactly the same way that Skye determines that Shamans do, once again proving that Shamanism & the Old Religion are one!

In DEOSIL DANCE Issue 17, & in THE HARMONICS OF WICCA, I made correlations between the tradition of North American Shamanism, & the Old religion of Albion, this has been commented upon by members of both tradition as being correct with the similarities drawn being so obvious. In fact I know at least one person who is a member of a Shamanic group who is seeking admittance to Wicca after acknowledging that the two are inter related.

To conclude, Wicca is the shamanism of the lands of Albion, Cymru, Alba, Kernow Eire etc etc, whether in a Celtic or Saxon sense, it transcended the tribal system & developed in the village communities, with the so called wise ones taking on the traditional roles of the wise one of the tribe. This transition is still going forward & entering into The New Age. As such the shamanism of these lands is alive & well in the followers of the Old Religion in these lands, & is seen as still being an active force within the lives that it touches.

There is one thing that we do have to be aware of, & that is, that this essential force should bee seen as being exactly what it is, & not be associated with even more dubious titles, designed to confuse the uninitiated (& the would be oppressors), or even worse, to try & falsely ally pagan beliefs complete within themselves, & not in need of any additional credibility, which will fail the essential examinations that will of course be given to them in the course of time.

To avoid a critical expose of a later time of 'Invented religions', we have to keep to our pagan ethic of KEEPING PURE OUR HIGHEST IDEALS- & STRIVING EVER TOWARDS THEM!

THE USE OF NEW MAGICKAL TOOLS

Within Wicca & other pagan orientated groups, we are familiar with the 5 elemental tools as being the focal points to the equipment used, within the ritual as being representative of the elemental forces within the ritual.

These tools are;

Earth - Pentacle

Air - Wand

Fire - Sword

Water - chalice

Spirit - Athame.

The elemental association of this, I am personally happy with as I can relate to these individual correspondences *& can accept this as being a familiar feature within what has been classified as being the 'Western Mystery Tradition', which has often wrongly included Wicca. It is a universal concept & one that the majority of people are happy with.

The one big flaw with these tools, is that in essence they are cabbalistic in orientation, & are not tools that would be familiar to our ancestors within their magickal workings, simply because what we associate as Wiccan is not part of the 'Western Mystery tradition'.

Of course some of the above tools, our ancestor would be very familiar with ATHAME= Sacred Knife; CHALICE= sacred vessel, cauldron, etc; WAND= Staff etc, but what of the sword & the Pentacle, especially the Pentacle, this is a totally cabbalistic magickal ritual tool, & as such is an import within Wicca of an era after the 12th century (as a conservative estimate)

Tools that would have been familiar to our ancestors, may be frowned upon within Wiccan circles by some people as being 'Shamanic' in orientation, but, as we have already discussed earlier in this book, what is the problem with that!

Our ancestors of the Celtic, Saxon & Nordic tribes, that were the wise ones, were the shamans of their tribe, they worked with the spirit, they worked with the raised energy within their magickal creativity, why should we disregard tools of other cultures, after all, they may be tools that were familiar to our ancestors.

What I am of course saying, is not to disregard all your existing magickal tools, not one bit of it, after all a tool is only as good as the service that it gives, & there is no reason at all to suggest that simply because a pentacle is of a cabbalistic nature, that it could not give service within a pagan ritual, the athame, is a vital need for both our ancestors & ourselves.

What i am suggesting is that other tools be brought in to compliment those that we are already working with & are familiar with, in creating a new current of magickal working that would be more consistent with the spirit of our ancestors

Such tools would include things such as

Fans; Drums & rattles; Pipes; Bowls; Staves

These tools too can have a symbolic attachment to the nature of the elements, being part of their own composite make-up & relation to the elements accordingly becomes easy.

Air - **Fans**

Earth - **Drums & rattles**

Fire - **Pipes**

Water - **Bowls**

Spirit - **Staves**

Like all other magickal tools these new & additional tools cane be quite easily made by the wise one, using materials that are found in their natural environment, as shamans or wise ones of all cultures make their tools.

Fans -fans can be as simple as a dried birds wing, or a silk or paper fan of an oriental nature. the effect that a fan has upon the air is to disturb the current & to create a presence of its own, which carries the power of the instrument. Use a fan in conjunction with Incense for an effectual invocation or purification.

Burn the incense in a bowl before you, & when there is a steady column of smoke , scoop the smoke onto the fan & direct it wherever you choose. Purification using smoke & a fan is known as 'Smudging' to the North American Shamans & is an effective way in directing energy obtained through burning herbs, the presence of the burning herbs & the magick present in their smoke is one very beneficial way of bringing the energy into a situation.

Fans can also be used to channel healing energy towards a target or an individual, or to a certain part of the body,& are particularly effective within ceremonies towards this end.

Drums & rattles - the deep rhythmic effect that a drum has upon the subconscious is very effective & is thought of as being the heartbeat to the Earth.

A Frame Drum, is a simple drum of a skin stretched over a hoop of wood. these may be made or bought, as Bodhrans in most acoustic music shops.

The beater, or beaters that should be considered are beaters that have been padded at the end to give a dull impact. Experiment using the different beats & rhythms, seeing the effect that they have upon the subconscious.

Trance work can be obtained from steady drumming, with a timing of 130 beats per minute being recommended by many drummers for deep trance work.

Personally I feel that it is different beats for different people, I have found that listening to my own heart & following the beat of that is most effective for me in obtaining astral gateways & in controlling a situation where I am present both as a guardian & as the controller of a situation

Pipes - A smoking pipe could be considered to be an essential fire altar, with the spirit of fire resident within the pipe.

It is the ingestion of smoke from a sacred pipe that helps with trancework using teacher plants that have a reputation for being gateways. There is a strict code of ethics regards the sacred uses of pipes & herbs, sacred to many cultures, these are entered into in my book A SHAMANIC HERBAL SACRED PLANTS - SACRED WAYS.

Bowls - Bowls are symbols of the Goddess, wombs of the Mother, they can be used ritualistically akin to the chalice, A sacred bowl is is essence the cauldron of Ceredwenn, the cauldron of inspiration, inspiration can be achieved in many ways.

Water meditations, or scrying can be achieved by filling your bowl with water, & gazing into the surface to obtain visions. Bowls can be of any material that you choose, Glass, pewter & other metals, or , as I have found, earthenware, which is an excellent representative for the sexual & reproductive energies of the Great Earth Mother.

My own earthenware bowl, a small cauldron was given to me as a present from another Coven, as a gift for the ritual that I had just performed with them, as well as sharing with them my own insights & inspirations. Battered & chipped it may be but to me it is truly a cauldron of knowledge & inspiration!

Bowls are also perfect incense burners, within a ritual or ceremony, & can be used for both purposes.

Staves - Your stave could be looked upon as another wand, as a passive tool of defence that is used in ceremonies for action.

It could be as simple or as decorated as you choose, but should in some way reflect the spirit of the occasion or cycle that you are progressing through.

Within ceremonies & rituals concerning more than 2 people, it can be used as a 'talking stick', that is , as a symbol of democratic authority at that time & place.

Talking sticks are used within discussions to give all the opportunity to inject their own ideas into the ceremony.

Whilst a person is holding the talking stick, none may break into what that person is saying, nor interrupt or contradict, it is that persons time space & power that is important, & for this reason, it is the building up of the energies into that stave that creates the spirit that resides within it.

As a form of wand, the stave can be used to direct energy in a way exactly the same as a wand,to focus, direct & channel the energy to a desired end.

Complimentary use of these tools alongside what is already regarded as 'Standard issue' brings the realms of experimentation within ritual into a greater perspective.

Boundaries between what is acceptable & what is not must be determined by the practitioner & only by the practitioner, it being their own responsibility as to the nature & effect of the ceremony or ritual.

It is important that the same respect be given for any 'alternative tools', to that of the already established collection of Ritual magickal tools, because a concept is new to you does not mean that it will not work, its all a matter of keeping an open mind & experimenting to find out what does work for you & what does not.

In this way you will be walking a sacred path, that has been walked by many in times past & will be walked by as many in times to come.

NON RITUAL MAGICK

Structured Ritual magick, using a collection of elemental magickal tools, & combining it with planetary significance has become combined with Pagan expressions of magickal ceremonies over a period of years from the middle ages onward.

If we go back further to a time when mankind only understood the power of nature around him, when he lived a very simplified lifestyle, often in caves or rough shelters, possessing only that which he stood up in, & the only equipment that he carried was equipment that was essential to his existence, especially if he lived a nomadic lifestyle, then the excess baggage of the unnecessary would only hinder him on his progress, & this is the same today.

What was important to him, was the here & now- not tomorrow, not next week, for there was no weeks, Tomorrow depended upon whether the great Sun God decided to shine upon the Earth, thus giving them a tomorrow. There was a great fear connected with this ancient belief of the here & now.

It was only in the later times that the significance of which planet was important at a particular time, & to what influence such had on a situation, to our most ancient of ancestors the effects of the outer planets were not known, the understanding to these people, were what was in their immediacy, & this was the Earth, & The Sun & The Moon, & around these three everything revolved .

To our more ancient of ancestors that the power of the here & now mattered, for there was no forward planning.

As with the energy raised within a primal scream, so was the energy raised within these rituals of sympathetic magick. If the purpose of the ritual was a kill for food, the shamans of old enacted the moves that they hoped to make moving in for the kill, practising their moves, raising their energies ready for what they hoped would happen. It was hunger that inspired them into generating the energy to put into their magick, & they did not go out, with any doubt in their minds that their magick would fail. they went out knowing that they were to make a kill, their magick had been performed & it would succeed.

Sometimes of course it did not, but this was not down to magick, this was down to the failure of the people involved, someone had either been disrespectful to the energies, or someone had doubted the magick, both which were not allowed, & great taboos or superstitions were built up around magickal acts, thus increasing the positive aspects of them & removing any aspects of doubt from within them!.

The wise ones of old did not consider themselves to be indulging in a ritual that was external to a situation, what they were doing, was creating a ceremony in which they could live their lives within a sacred manner, creating a spirit around them that would make them harmonious with the animal that they were preparing to kill, for the benefit of the Tribe.

As this was not ritual to our ancestors, but more of a ceremonial linking in, so as we develop, must we, get used to a ceremonial linking rather than the intensity of a ritual.

To raise energy to a Pagan should come as one of the most natural things possible to them, as it was to our ancestors,

This natural energy raising is the pre runner of what we may describe as Non-Ritual magick, that is magick that can be demanded upon will rather than waiting for certain planetary times, conditions etc, which is which cabbalistic magick asks practitioners to do, by waiting until certain aspects are more favourable, & until corresponding aspects align themselves..

Of course there is absolutely nothing wrong in this, & waiting for magickal alignments is a great lesson of patience, & is something that a raw beginner should become accustomed too, as magick as being results upon demand is going to prove a grave disappointment to everyone!

Especially the person who expects it!

A more easy to handle concept of Non ritual magick must be the magick of the mind, understanding the natural energies & making the desired end result become a mental achievement rather than as a physical manifestation.

The concept of Non ritual magick is a very simple one.

Magick exists, therefore it is!

Our potential for creating Magick exists
- therefore it is possible!

Our will to do that magick & to bring it into effect exists
- therefore it is!

Magick is the bringing together of natural elemental energies, into creating an effect, either for positive or negative ends.

We do not need a circle to cast a spell, to do a tarot reading, or to heal somebody. We all have that capability & potential within our own bodies, & it works because it exists & we exist & if we understand this potential then we acknowledge that it exists & therefore it works.

A perfect example of this is seen within an often come across situation. A Friend of ours asked for help in getting a sum of money owed to him returned. He really needed this money & he was really angry that he was being outdone at not having the money, Dianne said she would do something to help.

An immediate spell, was set into action & the money arrived the very next day! Right, sceptics would of course say that the cheque was in the post, & the magickal act was not needed as the cheque was already in the post, but who performed the magickal act, Dianne or the Friend?

The magickal act was not the spell cast for there was no spell cast as such it was more of a recognition of a situation!). The magickal act was the cry for help, through the anger of being deprived what was rightly his, he was building up this pressure for days & days & something just gave, that something was the forceful release of power which made the third party come to his senses & pay what was owing.

The cheque being in the post was the result to the magick being brought to a head by the discussion with Dianne, & the asking for help, this was the culmination of the non ritual magick being performed by both our friend & Dianne! .

Circles are very useful in having a unifying & forceful effect, though as we have already discussed to do one every time one needs some power, at the drop of a hat, would leave the practitioner absolutely exhausted. A truly cast circle with the true pulling together of elemental forces leaves the practitioner mentally shattered & it takes time to recover from rituals, if correctly performed, as opposed to the showbiz circles that we see so often, that is why to do one everytime one needs power is not a good idea, not is it needed, the magick is all around!

Look at how things are in what 'Modern, usually Christianised, western mankind'' may consider to be the 'primitive' cultures as described earlier, as well as other 'Stone age cultures' that are still around today, where the activities of the wise one, witch doctor or medicine man, is tantamount to the security of the tribal situation.

Whenever a spell needs to be cast, whenever healing needs to be performed, whenever a problem needs to be solved, it is the tribal spiritual leader who officiates.

he does not say, sorry, cannot heal your child of fever today, the moon is not in the necessary portion of the sky, & I have no red candles to help you succeed with your crops!

The job needs to be done & the wise one gets to it & does the job, he works with what is around him, at whatever time he is at, & because it is he (or she) that is doing it, the rest of the tribe agree that it is right, & proper & will work.

It is two things that make magick fail

Doubt & disrespect!

Doubt- in that the person doing the magick, has not done it correctly, has not got the right things around themselves to do it properly(!)

Disrespect - In that the person doing the magick, is seen as being not qualified to do it properly! That the person doing the magick does not have the full respect of the community, therefore is not seen as being powerful within that community.

If doubt sets in, then the magick will fail - because like a seed, if a seed is sown into barren ground, then it will not take, for the ground will not nourish the seed, will not give the seed what it needs in generating the energy to become a plant.

So it is with the relationship of a wise one, & we can take the tribal situation, as being the Coven, with the leader of the coven Priest, priestess of facilitator if you so choose, as being the guiding light within that coven, they are the wise one of that community & as such are called upon to officiate at ceremony & ritual. Called upon to teach the magickal ways to others & called upon to establish disputes. If we look at modern societies labelling service (available free of charge to all who are gullible!), we can see that a modern coven, is a primitive society!

Because of this, we have the status within the coven as a close knit community of the leader as being a wise one. Whatever they do, has to be correct; has to be with the full approval of the rest of the group, & for the greater part has to be seen to work.

I do not want to be accused of generating bullshit, or of instigating hype, there is far too much of this, but there is also far to much of a ritualised bullshit that too many people perform, that is the over importance of ritual within a magickal situation, for it is not needed.
What is needed, is competent people who can run groups well, who do perform magick for the community, who do teach, & who are taught. It does not matter if that person does not do it to the script of a certain book, if that person is performing magick for that group, & that group believe in that magick, then it will work.

It will work for two reasons.

Natural energy & respect

Natural energy in the fact that a belief in the powers of the elements as being manifestations of the dual aspected Male /Female unity of the Lord & LADY? Great Spirit? are at work in whatever circumstance is needed, whether that is in a ritual or in the head of a wise one.

Respect - the magick is working because the respect for the wise one is manifested throughout the group. they know that the wise one is powerful, they know that if they have said that something will happen it will. If a healing spell will work, it will, that is non negotiable.

This is magick in action. the action that the magickal current has upon the group or society. It is the old adage of giving someone a bad name, if so many people do it, it sticks, regardless of the truth. So it is with magick, if a person is deemed to be competent & capable, then they are BUT it is not regardless of the truth, for as magick has a unifying & discriminatory force, it is the force of our deities in action, if someone is lying, or bullshitting, or saying something that is not correct, the energy that is the magickal current will not work through them,

BECAUSE THEY HAVE THE TWO THINGS WITHIN THEM WHICH WILL NOT MAKE THE MAGICK WORK, DOUBT & DISRESPECT!

To think of something in a magickal context is to believe in its existence. belief is the keyword, for if you do not believe that it will happen, it wont. This belief is manifested through the belief in the Lord & Lady, I am amazed at the amount of Pagans that I have met, who consider the Lord & lady as being an allegorical synthesis of other established religious views. The God as being a Jesus; Moses: Mohammed; Buddha image that we can attune to. the Goddess as being a Virgin Mary; Fatima; image, one of virginal, exestentional properties.
    This is not the Lord & Lady of Creation, this is modern thinking of an ancient concept, & what you will get with such an irrational & complacent & compromising view, is again doubt!
Do not doubt that these deities exist, for if you do doubt that this manifestation of the   magickal energies of nature fails to exist, then for you it wont, for you it will never work.

Your own doubt has already killed off the seed of creation that you have sowed on barren soil, through your own doubting.

To think of an effect to be caused within a magickal manner will make that action become reality within your own thinking. This can be through a spell, working with elements if you so desire, but again, this is only if you are happy with such a technique. To acknowledge the existence of something is to give it life, & to give it life means that it is your responsibility & karma. It is a part of you just as a conventional spell would be, no magickal equipment is needed, no spells need to be said, no chants need to be spoke. the simple acceptance of a situation is enough to give it power.

Let me quote an example of this that happened;

I was driving home very early one morning with my car loaded with luggage, not that anything about this situation was illegal, everything was in order, but to a policeman it looked suspicious. As I passed a parked police car, I was speeding quite considerably, as I wanted to get home before dawn. As I looked behind me, the police car had pulled out, & was not only following me, but was flashing the blue lights at me to stop. With what I can only describe as a tired & anguish yell, at my bad luck, at my stupidity for speeding, at the time that would be wasted with all the formalities that this would entail, I started to stop, In my mind, I wished the Police car was somewhere else, & directed my thoughts in that direction. the next thing that I could remember was the police car speeding very fast past me, overtaking & speeding off into the night.

Afterwards I analysed the situation that I had experienced.

1; Had I aroused the Policeman's attention by breaking a law - yes, I was speeding past him, he could not have failed to notice me, as there was no one else around.

2; Was the Police Car actually chasing me - yes he was, the light was flashing, indicating me, to slow down, there was no one else about on the road.

3; What changed his mind?

The only conclusion that I can reach, is that his mind was changed by other events, circumstances etc being brought to his attention.

Whether that was my magickal intervention, or another matter, I do not know, but for my part, I know that it was the manner in which I was conducting my own thinking, in a way to influence this third party into taking an alternative action that would leave me, free to do my will, which was getting home before dawn.

Of this I am definite in my observations, & have no doubt at all that the magick manifested was working through me, & worked for me!

To conclude this chapter of non ritual magick, It is enough to say that the wise one knows how to create a magickal environment & through past experiences within the circle, brings those experiences forth, through past knowledge & understanding's of the interactive magick within the circle, & to bring this energy through their own presence, as being a balance of the energies, & to manifest & direct this energy into directing it towards an end intention.

Again, Magick exists, therefore it is

That magick can be used, therefore it has been!

WORLDS OF CONSCIOUSNESS

Whenever we perform an action upon the Earth plane, we have to be conscious that such an action through its cause & effect, will not only touch the lives of other people upon the Earth plane, but also, that such effects will be felt upon other planes of consciousness.

Within the Cabbala, different planes of existence are manifested upon the Tree of Life; Within Nordic cultures it is the concept of the World Tree Yggdrasil & its component parts as the tree as the central pillar of the universe.

Our sacred circle, that is the circle of Magick, is not a world separate from the world of reality that we live 70% of our lives in, but is rather a focal point for the magickal energy to manifest in our daily lives.

Being a gateway between the worlds of man & Spirit, is not divorced from the world it is very much a part of it, & part of the individual worlds within us, through the circle where we can grow to learn things, we can take on the teachings of each of the individual quarters in such a way that we can not only benefit from them ourselves, but of benefit by them for other people.

As the Shamans of ancient times transcended the planes of existence, to descend into the underworld, to Transcend onto higher levels of consciousness, so can we, with the aid of a 'map', venture into the worlds of element to assert for ourselves the teachings & learnings of each of the elements.

Sacred maps have been used in a magickal context since very early times, mans manifestation of universal realities into a two dimensional object is a common practise to try & achieve a dominance over the forces that are being represented in the map.

Maps from other traditions include, the very familiar TREE OF LIFE of the cabbalistic tradition, often represented as a two dimensional object, with ten circles, paths linking all 10 spheres, with a hidden sphere, of chaos as being the eleventh.

This is of course valid, when realising that the concept is but a two dimensional one, but, when the map becomes a three dimensional map, then it opens worlds out beyond any parameters & confines that a two dimensional image gives.

If we consider the circle as being our 'map' into the realms of the elements & the energies, lessons & teachings of each element, we can then plot our future development upon each of the elements & at each position that we reach within the circle.

This can be done either through ritual or ceremony, or more naturally through establishing a rapport with that element upon its own terms In other words, if we wish to equate with the Energies of water, then we immerse ourself in that element & open ourself out to the energies & teachings that such an experience gives us.

Likewise with the element of air, to go onto a high hilltop when a wind is blowing & feel the currents that are passing over you & through you, you will experience the power & sensuality of the elements by establishing contact with them in a natural habitat far more than if you were performing such contacts within the confines of a ritual within a temple, which may be your only alternative, but is far from equation with the element in its raw & essential state.

I think possibly one of the true concepts of structured presence within the universe, is mirrored within our own circles, working in a way of cycles. To the Amerinds these were medicine Wheels, to the Tibetans they are Thangkas, to Wiccans they are the Magickal circle.

If we expand the circle that we know of being an elemental circle, & expand upon its power, in that the direction that it touches reflects the energy of that direction & its effects upon the powers that it touches, including yourself.

Personally, I would choose to view the concept of other world consciousness as a four dimensional object as is the earth, but within the realms of a circle, as a three dimensional circle This may be difficult to understand, but let me try & illustrate.

The First Dimension.

_____

That which we know,   *a single plane*

we know of the existence of this the Earth plane, because we are here, it is a known fact. We could not deny the existence of this plane for if we did, we deny our own existence upon it.

The second dimension

That which we understand   *A dual plane*
Within Wicca & other esoteric philosophies we are given the understanding of the Astral planes, as being a place of magickal manifestation, that of ascension & descension from the astral to the earth Plane.

The third Dimension

That which we accept   *A third depth*

From the astral planes we have a choice, do we ascend higher to become one with the divinity that we are essentially part of, or do we once again descend upon the Earth plane to take part in further incarnations. This is a plane of decision, & we, as responsible participants in the universe, have to accept that our decision is the one that matters to us - & other lives that we touch within our existence.

The Fourth Dimension

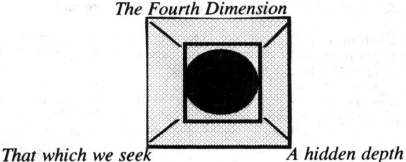

That which we seek   *A hidden depth*

This is the dimension that we cannot see, we can feel its energy, because we know that it is there, we can feel the power coming from it. **THIS IS THE REALM OF MAGICK!**

This is the realm of deity, of the essential power that is venerated within Wicca & associate pagan circles as God & Goddess.

What must be seen from this crude two dimensional example of a four dimensional theory, is that all are interlinked, the one, two, three & four dimensional concepts are not divorced from each other, but are to be found upon the Earth plane each as part of each other.

This goes a long way to explain why, Wiccans & pagans do not consider the concept of deity, in some form of judeo exestentional being, separate from the earth. The Earth is our Goddess & God - we must take care of them!

But, if we view the earth as being totally self sufficient for all sacred needs, then how can we view the importance of other planets stars etc that are within our universe. WE can because they affect even from afar, because life upon the Earth is pliable, being on the whole between 50 & 90% water, we are affected by outer influences, both physically & mentally. It therefore goes without saying that other planets affect us in the same way on different levels, which is of course the basis of the science of astrology

If we look at this in a manner that befits the human race - selfishly! We can take the role that what is important to us, as beings of The earth, is the things that touch us directly, that is all of the manifestations of the four planes, & their composite parts.

The Earth in itself is complete, complete with our own unique form of divinity & as such, must be at the centre of' our' universe, for it is the things that matter to us personally.

This, is not to say, that the effects of the other planets are not important to us, as astrology has pointed out, the influence of the other planetary influences upon the inhabitants of the Earth is important to such, & within astrology, we view the earth as being central to the astrologers wheel. The horizon is taken as being the ascendant, i.e.; what has ascended within the heavens above the axis of the earth that is dawn/dusk. So it is with the midheaven, that which is directly above us, affects us.

We must take the concept of the earth as being central to our universe, as dwellers of this earth, but, we must also take into consideration the effects that other planetary influences have upon our nature.

What may be seen to be a selfish concept of, we are important, we are at the centre of all this, is not down to human arrogance, for when I say we, I do not mean just humans, I mean;

My two legged brothers & sisters - the human world
My Four legged Brothers & sisters - the animal world
My Two winged Brothers & sisters - the bird world
My Finned Brothers & sisters - the fish world.
My Brothers & sisters of nil or many limbs - the insect world
My brothers & sisters of the Plant world
My Brothers & sisters of the Mineral world
My Brothers & sisters of the Otherworlds!

We all have our roles to play in this our world, a world for all of us, created from the very bones blood & tissue of the Great earth Mother, our Goddess., & her consort, the Horned one, & we are all part of this Great Earth even after death. yes even after Death, consider the fact that the earth is totally self contained, very little goes out & very little comes in!

When we die we, one way or another become one with the earth again, as we are returned to it, is not our physical body replenishing the Earth with a percentage of the nutrients that we have taken out of it in the timespan of our living time upon the earth. We become one with our deities, being the earth & as we ascend higher consciousness, we ascend to higher levels of magickal attainment via our essential spirit, which as Physics tells us, energy cannot be killed, just changed, then as we die, our essential spirit (soul, astral, call it what you will), transcends to develop further, & ye shall know & love them again!

As is our interaction with the Earth, then So it is with other planets,(& let us make sure we understand the concept of what we mean by a planet), each world, that interjects with ours, has a spirit & possibly a population of its own, because we have not got the olfactory senses to understand about its population, does not give us the right to deny it. each planet within the universe, is a living being, like every living being upon the Earth plane.

If we view the Earth Plane as a universe for the lives involved, then we must view the universe as being a plane for the lives also involved, that is, the planetary life. So as the earth is important to us, & as the planets are resonating a power of their own that we can feel, so it is vice versa, all having a place & power within each others aura.

This goes a long way to explaining the role of The Earth within the universal worlds & each planets importance upon each other, but what of the other worlds that exist within the four dimensions.

What we may consider to be a world, or a realm, is a state

of consciousness, that we can attune to & work with to develop ourselves & our magickal energies. These other worlds can be classified as;

The living world; the world in which we conduct two-thirds of our life in. The conscious world

The Dreaming world; the world in which we conduct one third of our life in. The unconscious world

Along with these two worlds which have their roles within the first & second dimensions, we have other worlds that interweave their energies with our two earth worlds, & reflect their energies upon the further 2 dimensions.

These worlds are;

1: The creative world;

2: The destructive world

3: the sexual world

4: the working world

5: the world of Myth

6: the world of Logic

7: The thinking world

8: The world of love

It is with the interaction of these worlds upon either our Living or dreaming world that creates the many & varied manifestations that we can work with on magickal levels.
For example within our Living world, we can indulge ourselves in all of the above, in our waking state, but what about in our dreaming world, is any of this possible?

the answer of course is yes!

Simply because we are in a different state of consciousness, does not mean that we are not capable of doing any of the activities that exist within the eight worlds of being.

In our dreaming state we are able to be far more creative, far more destructive, far more intense about whatever we choose, because the only restriction that is placed upon us in the dreamstate is the restrictions that we choose to take for our own.

Otherworlds all have keys,symbols or expressions that allow us to enter these worlds for the purpose of learning of the concepts of these worlds & how we can use them, relate to them & adapt them for your own usage.

When Odin descended to Niflheim, he returned with the Runes, symbols of wisdom & storytellers within their own right. the key that the hero Odin used for this transition was the key of self sacrifice, that of putting his life on the line for the obtaining of the wisdom that he returned with - this is the essence of otherworld keys, that of the personal interrelation between the person, his goal & his journey to that goal dependent upon which plane the goal or achievement lies within.

This is the key to otherworld transcending, that of which is important & relevant for you, no one can explain this to you, no one can do it for you, this is the essence of the sacred journey, its all yours & its all up to you!

WORKING WITH THE LIGHT?

When working with a concept of natural magick, there are many energies that we can work with & use for our own purposes.

Within Wicca, we view the concept of deity as being a dualistic concept of Male/Female energy, manifesting itself as God & Goddess.

This concept of a dualistic polarity is also to be found in the natural manifestations of elemental forces, of Fire Water, Earth, Air & Spirit. To this end, each element is not ascribed an individual gender, but rather, as polarity of gender manifesting this gender through individual aspects of the element

Take for example the concept of water, it is to be found in many forms, but according to each form & the action of the form, they are either Male or female, The Sea is Female, But a Geyser is male. Likewise with fire, a volcano can be a manifestation of a feminine energy, whilst a sacred fire at a Lammas to celebrate the feast of Lugh/Llew will be Male.

It would be far to easy to work through this & give a listing for each element, but if you cannot relate to these concepts as I see them, it will not work for you (again Doubt & Distrust - negative energy!). You would be far better working through yourself & finding the individual aspects that you can relate to & use within your own magick.

It is through the manifestations of natural energy that deities emerged, as being visualisation of the individual energy or energies of a personification or embodiment of an aspect that was desirous to be in contact with.

Other energy forces are of course the Planetary forces that affect our everyday lives, each planet having a corresponding energy that we can relate to, My book TRADITIONAL WICCA deals with the aspect of planetary invocation & the relationship of correspondences with the planetary forces.

It must be stressed that when using any of these energy forces, it need not only be in ritual or ceremony, to acknowledge the beneficial actions of these forces is enough to recognise the effect that they can have upon you, upon your life & upon your magickal workings, to direct your thoughts or channel your energies emotions or feelings through these powers is enough to bring them into effect for yourself or for any goal or ambition that you are driving towards.

Taking this concept a stage further, we must also note that with the elemental wheel, of

Earth

Water   *Air*

Fire

That each of the elements have a dualistic gender, then we must also relate to each of them as having a positive & negative gender, so therefore, we have several manifestations of each element given below

	MALE	FEMALE	POSITIVE	NEGATIVE
EARTH				
WATER	Geysers	Pools	Rivers	Ice
FIRE				
AIR				

The example of water has been given above, I leave it to the individual to attune their own associations, & of course the above opinion for water is merely my own interpretation, insert your own if they differ from mine (which I hope they do!)

TOWARDS A NEW AGE

Wicca is changing, it has to to survive. The changes that need to be made are open to us all, the first change is a change in perspective, Wicca is for all, the philosophies, lessons to be taught & the lifestyle of living in a magickal harmonious way are or should be open to all who wish to follow this personal philosophy.

We need to change. the basic belief of the Primal deities has not changed, since the time, when we, as our ancestors lived in caves.

We no longer live in caves, we no longer are afraid of the dark, but there are still other matters which concern us, & which need equating to our magickal & religious philosophies, we like them are not divorced from the reality of this world that we live in & as such we all need to be equated with each other so that all is balanced, all is well & all is relevant.

Wicca is an old Religion, true, but one that is very welcome in the New Age for the philosophies it has to teach are relevant to all, no matter in which age we live in, Wicca & Wiccan philosophies are adaptable

We are now entering into a new age, the enlightened age of Aquarius, an age of individuality, free thinking, free expression, freedom. This will be a bold & brave new age for all those embracing the spirit of such a concept. As a new age philosophy, Wicca has a place within this New Age & should be ready to take its place within it.

In the 60's, everyone was looking for significant astrological markers for the dawning of the New Age;

"When the Moon is in the Seventh House, & Jupiter aligns with mars. "
or so the song goes.

Entering the New Age will not be a case of looking at the calendar to find the New Age comes next Tuesday, the new age will emerge within a persons own understanding, when they become enlightened people, when they have been touched with the spirit of the enlightenment that the Earth is sacred

They will have been touched because they have opened themselves out to the influences that are all around them, like a child they have opened their arms & have been lifted.

Of course to many people, people with a monosyllabic attitude, the essential spirit of the New Age will go unseen, as it is not this that they are essentially searching for, & as such will miss the bus so to speak.

The dawn of the New age manifests itself in peoples spirit & not in any astrological alignment, the new age has begun, for it began a long while ago in the hearts of enlightened people who started to give the answers that a desperately dying twentieth century was craving for. These people for the greater part were considered mad, bad or generally undesirable.

These people are far to many to name, many are totally underestimated, totally misunderstood, & this is the mark of true enlightenment, when one is misunderstood, one does not rant & rave, one sits quietly for that person to finish what they are saying, whether it is right or wrong.

That person is then thanked for their opinion - this is enlightenment, the ability to see through the failings of the Human body & to seek the perfection that lies in the soul.

The road to hell may be paved with good intentions, if that is so, then perhaps the road to heaven is paved with misunderstandings!

To arrive at the concept of a New age is like a great spiritual spaceship, it will take only those who wish to embark upon its journey, away from decay & chaos towards a new dawn, a new dawn where all are equal, regardless of race, Sex, Creed, Colour, Age etc etc.

Those of us wanting to embark upon this mission must consider our futures very carefully indeed, for we will be caretakers of a new dawn, & as such have responsibilities towards that new dawn.

What we take with us into our own individual New Ages is very important, for as we live our lives now, this twilight of the Piscean age, with the dawn of the New Age breaking, shedding new light, we can see the rot & decay & harm that those, within the piscean age have created, to our fragile & gentle Mother Earth.

There is a saying ;
if you are not part of the solution - you are part of the Problem!'

This is very true, for if we cannot embrace the concept of entering into a new dawn in its totality, then we will be a problem to the fragile first stirrings of the New Age.

If we decide to take with us such things from the Old Age that we think that we are comfortable with, then we will stifle the essential current immediately.

Such things, as
Dogma, Hypocrisy, Sloth, Greed, uncompassionate behaviour, Inconsiderate attitude, Laziness, Intolerance

All of these concepts & many more are seen to be of a monotheistic or selfish nature, & in their very action will not allow the growth of a natural progressive action to take place.

That is why, we who would consider ourselves as caretakers of the New Age have to be aware of the dangers of carrying any of the old age traits with us, for if we do, we need not bother to attempt to harness the essential spirit that is the New Age, for we will not have even started to have learned the lessons of this Piscean age, & as such will infect the essential new spirit of the growing child that is the New Age.

The invitation is there, it is up to us to be able to carry forward into this dream our own philosophies & understandings of Wicca & what we perceive it to be, so that in the mad rush for recognition The Old ways will not be left out.

HIERARCHY OR LEADERSHIP

Recently I had one or two private letters concerning my review of 'Witchcraft - a Tradition renewed' that featured in the reviews column of Deosil Dance 24. Many people thought that I was rebelling against the coven system of Wicca, I was not, what I was saying is that the dogma of certain aspects of what may be described as a strict coven has been emerging within Wicca. If Wicca is to re-establish itself as a Living religion to the majority of the community that we live in, & to re-assert itself as being a legitimate belief within the world arena.

I was not inferring that Covens are old Hat, but pointing out that a new approach is evolving to bring the Teachings of the Old ways to a wider audience of people, & The reintroduction of personalised ways of workings, known to our ancestors, rather than repeating parrot fashion other peoples words of devotion in ritual - the old ways come from the heart not a book!

This was my main complaint with the book, it was not seen as a beginning process, but as a strictly laid out way that was non negotiable, & this is not the way.

Wicca is not anti-establishment or pro Dogma, true Wicca allows people to think for themselves, to assess their role to play in the great scheme of things, without fearing an oppressive attitude from someone who they fear (as most Christians fear their ministers, when they differ slightly from the party line!)

Some people have got the wrong idea about my stance on the role of the Coven within todays Wiccan/Pagan movement. As it was impossible to do justice to a complex subject like this, in such a small space as a book review, I will go deeper into this subject here, - as being my own opinion.

I must say at the outset, why I feel that Wicca, as it has developed over the last 30 years,is now diversifying away from a 'Strict' Coven system. I feel that this is happening now, because things of a Pagan nature are more in the open. I can recall, when I was looking for a coven to join back in the late 70's, there was nothing open & available. The only magazine that was available was 'prediction', which at the time did not carry advertisements for Covens. I had to rely upon word of mouth, & eventually when I did get to meet the Priest & Priestess of the Coven, there attitude was what I could only consider hostile!

However, eventually, they did admit me to the coven & I was duly initiated & trained - But, any outside contact away from the coven that I was a member of, & associate sister covens, was strictly advised against. The reason being was so not to confuse the initiates with conflicting ideas of other people!

This was only 13 years ago, & you can see the level of secrecy of such groups then, with the openness that we enjoy today.

Nowadays however I am happy to say that things are considerably more out in the open, & covens are around & happy to talk to people about their beliefs, but with my own experience of strict covens, & with relating to other peoples problems of strict secretive covens, I have noted problems with such.

Problems such as; The 'High' Priest & Priestess not actually being initiated & starting the group to satisfy their own ego's .... Secret groups being not what they seem, Satanists etc, masquerading as Pagans!.... Secret groups using the group for an excuse for sexual licentiousness.

Within open groups, or groups run by well known Wiccans/Pagans etc, none of this exists, as there is too much credibility to be lost by the people running the group. People with something to hide usually keep their beliefs, groups etc secret also!

Now I must say, that this is in a minority, but it does happen, & has caused a great deal of distress to people getting involved!

I am sure that most people will agree, that this is the kind of problems that we should be getting away from, & with open groups etc we are, for we are also open to question, & we have either to put up or shut up! With an open group their is no bullshit with the usual cop out often given to seekers, 'That its not yet right for you to know that' as the answer to a question that the teacher does not know the answer to, but is far to egotistical to admit that!

If we examine Covens around the world, we see some very definite differences, take the USA for Instance, which has a higher percentage of covens per capita, than the British Isles.

Covens in the USA work because the level of commitment from the people involved is so high, it is the members of a coven that make it work. The Priests & Priestesses of such groups have a respect, that I am sorry to say is not seen to be given in the British Isles, In fact, Priests & Priestesses here are sadly taken for granted by other coveners.

In the USA, Priests & Priestesses are maintained by Coven fee's of usually a tenth of a persons wage. In these lands such a concept would not be accepted or tolerated, because, people expect everything to be given to them,, without a mutual exchange in return, of help, etc. many is the complaint of Priests & priestesses here in the British isles, that coven members attend meetings, eat, drink & be merry, without any contribution their part - they wont even consider washing dishes, let alone bringing food to share!
To many people the concept of accepting fee's for teaching is a repulsive idea, & I for one am aware of that, for the concept of bringing Mammon into a circle as in the ability to pay governing wisdom, This leaves the door wide open for abuse from unscrupulous people who see a quick profit to be made. Enlightenment never comes through a cheque book, but then it doesn't also come from a Bankrupt Priestess unable to carry on her work, because of the financial difficulties she has been placed under by people taking advantage!

In America, (& I am not setting the American way of life as utopia, far from it - but they do have a greater level of commitment from the people involved!) where Group organisers are paid a tithe, the commitment from the organisers view for the greater part anyway is heightened. They know that they have to act like spiritual advisers, priests, teachers etc from any other culture. They have to be on call 24 hours a day for spiritual guidance, advice, comfort, they know they have to be capable of doing the job, & doing it well, they know that they have to arrange rituals, arrange workshops etc, usually in their own homes etc, & that those rituals better be right! For if they are not, they will soon get the reputation of being involved for all the wrong reasons!
We, within the Wiccan & pagan community do need a hierarchy, we all need teachers, & guides, & people to learn from, who have learned from experience themselves. What we do not

need is the egotism & the hype that many unscrupulous people try to impress others within a Wiccan context with. For all we are doing is leaving the door wide open for others, newly joined to Wicca & paganism to be hurt by

As pupils within a group, who are learning about the group etc, a system of levels of achievement is needed, like the degree systems of Wicca, so what if they are based upon masonic principles, they work well, in showing the aspiring student that there is a goal to be achieved, that it is worth sticking with it, when things get tough. Degrees or title should not be used as a means of pulling rank, for that smacks of egotism. All are equal, Neophyte & Priestess. What students need to realise is that not everyone will be a Priest or Priestess. For these roles are a vocation, a calling & as such not everyone is called to this role. Remember all Wiccans are Pagans, but not all pagans are Wiccans.

If we view Wicca & Covens & groups within Wicca, as the teaching capacity for the Priesthood, as it should be, then we would be getting near to the respect that the Hierarchy of such afford. Wicca is not anarchy, it is hard but rewarding work, & not everyone is cut out for it!

Within a coven or group situation, we do need leaders, who can take that group from a normal state of reality & transcend the astral worlds into a greater more heightened supersense that is needed for magick. This within Wicca & Paganism, is a genuine & definite need.

Most of all, what is needed is respect, respect of other peoples paths, traditions, levels of achievement, & even respect of other peoples personalities -

I think the concept of 'walking in another mans moccasins' to be totally overplayed - may I suggest "sleeping in another persons bed to be more in line with our fertility status, what it loses in the translation, it makes up for in reality!

THE WAY OF THE WARRIOR

All Pagans follow a path that was to our ancestors, the path of life, the way in which life itself was conducted, there was no differentiation between work, play, & beliefs, they all existed hand in hand.

Whenever a situation arose to challenge those beliefs, or to challenge that way of life, a decision was taken.

Was the challenge allowed to be taken place, to have that way of life suppressed - was another tribe allowed to come & take by force anything that was precious to the home tribe? Were they allowed to come & murder, & wreak havoc?

The answer is of course no!

Tribes were extended families, each one defensive of the other members of the tribe, true there were inter tribal arguments, & these were normally settled within the tribe, but when any other tribe challenged or confronted that tribe, they were united.

In our history as a Pagan nation, there have been many battles fought & many lives lost, by people defending what they hold precious.

This is part of our Pagan heritage the defence of what we hold as sacred!

The way of the warrior is the way of defence. Defence of what we hold to be sacred, to place our own safety on the line if it means defending what we hold to be sacred.

To Pagans today, what we hold sacred, is our beliefs, our lands may have been taken from us by force, newer religions may have come to disfigure our sacred old Gods & Goddesses turning them into demons,; but we, as a Pagan community still hold strong our beliefs in the old ways, & as such should be prepared to defend those beliefs, as our ancestors of old defended theirs.

One of the greatest problems that face todays Pagans is the process known among minority groups as 'Coming Out'.

Coming out entails coming out into the open, being prepared to admit to the world "Yes, I am Pagan. Pagan & proud!" This is a very hard step to take for once you have taken it there is no turning back, it is a public admission of your faith, which for many people, they may have kept hidden for so very long.

Once you have come out & admitted to the world that you are Pagan, you must be prepared to substantiate that claim by being prepared to tell people exactly what being a Pagan is all about. For this, you not only have to be correct in what you say, for any misunderstandings that you have will only enlarge with each extra telling that will be relayed to a third party, so the non Pagan public who you have told, will be pressing ahead with a misunderstanding, which is not good for the Pagan faiths.

To help you come out & admit that you are a Pagan, in the rear of this book, is a leaflet, 'WHAT IS A PAGAN' this will help you get your point over, you can photocopy it & distribute it as you wish.

Many people who are Pagan prefer not to use the word Pagan when they explain to others what their beliefs are. If confronted by authority, many people use the inevitable cop out of Agnostic / Atheist or No Religion. This is not only a cop out for yourself, but is also a cop out for the Pagan community who have come out into the open & are prepared to be counted for their beliefs.

With mainstream society being rather hung up, the choice of words that you use to tell people about your faith is important. Use the word 'Witch' & people will automatically consider you to be a devil worshipper. Use the word 'Wicca' & they will link you with basket weaving, if you follow other Pagan paths such as Nordic, Odinist, Celtic, Seax, Thelemic etc etc, a fuller explanation may not be allocated the time that it deserves in serving your faith to its best advantage , in gently getting the finer points of your belief over to a person who has probably never even heard of your belief.

To this end you may find it to be easier to use the word Pagan to encapsulate your beliefs, which, are , after all, Pagan

As the word Pagan is a word that is becoming more acceptable, this is a word that I choose to explain my religious beliefs, despite being an initiated Wiccan. It really is down to semantics, but is worth considering when coming out into the open as confusion will ultimately throw a persons line of thinking away from the essential interest & they will lose interest in what you are saying very quickly, choosing to believe only what they want to believe, which is generally not as accurate, as the truth would be - told in a manner that was simple & concise.

The word Pagan has been better recognised by the public of late, by the way in which people who are Pagan, show, that the use of the word Pagan is for a legitimate belief, rather than the sensationalist value of words such as 'Witch'. Please adopt this frame of mind when using the word Pagan, then you too will be seen as being 'Pagan & proud'

Authoritarian confrontation with your beliefs can include, hospitals, courts, solicitors, schools etc. On a personal level, I have had experience of telling these authorities that I was Pagan, their reactions were all on a non interest, basically they couldn't care less what belief you follow,, as long as it doesn't threaten the established status quo of, we will not consider bothering you , as long as you do not do anything that will make us sit up & take notice of you, or act in a way that makes us look stupid - basic human emotions really!.

When I was in hospital, a nurse asked me for my religion to fill in my forms, I told her I was a Pagan, & she put a dash where the answer was meant to go. I told her again I was a PAGAN, & she said that to her a Pagan had no belief, I told her quite firmly that a Pagan most certainly does have a belief & that is a valid religious path. She then begrudgingly wrote PAGAN in large letters over the line she had previously made. I thanked her. later that day, a vicar came round, had a look at the form at the bottom of my bed & said

" So you are a Pagan Eh! I must be important they've underlined it!"

When I had to swear an oath in court recently, I said I was a Pagan & chose to affirm, this is allowed, you do not have to swear on a Bible. If you are confronted on this matter, all you have to say is that as you are not a Christian, it is little circumstance to swear an oath on their holy book, likewise a Q'uran, & a Torah.

It is all a matter of sticking to your guns & standing firm insisting people acknowledge your belief as a Pagan as being valid.

Coming out is difficult, but is also rewarding, there is not the stigma that has been associated with Paganism in recent years, due entirely to people coming out & professing their pride in being Pagan.

In todays society, there is no benefit in hiding away, for if more Pagans did come out into the open, then the Pagan faiths will be more readily acceptable by a greater number of people.

If it is to be see that a Pagan is a perfectly normal member of the community who is no different to anyone else, in the basic day to day struggle of providing for you & your family, making sure that you can pay your way etc, then they will get to know you the person, rather than you the Pagan. When you do come out & admit to the truth of what you actually are the they will be far more ready to accept that Paganism is a serious belief & commitment for you & as such will be ready to accept that a Pagan is just a regular kind of person - just like you!

The Pagan way is a way of peace & tranquillity but it is also a path of truth, how can one admit to being true to oneself & ones deity when one cannot be truthful with those who come into contact with you in your everyday life.

As you & your path is touched by everything & everyone around you, so is everything & everyone around you, & who comes into contact with you, touched by you & your Pagan ways.

It is for this reason that you should 'keep pure your highest ideals & strive ever towards them' for your actions area reflection of what you are, a wise one, or a wise one to be. If you act stupidly, irrationally or selfishly, then the reflection of those negative actions manifest themselves upon the whole of the Pagan community.

This has been seen so often in the past with members of what is an alternative way of life, when something has happened, such as a group not clearing up after using a site, leaving bonfire remains etc, it leaves the door wide open for unfounded allegations to be aimed at you, simply because you have not considered the full implications of your actions, when manifest upon a greater audience many of whom, in the established society (that we who are part of an alternative way of life have broken away from) have a very critical attitude towards our beliefs way of life etc.

When you have the responsibility of your Pagan counterparts resting firmly upon your shoulders, you can see the responsibility that others are carrying for you - why should they burden themselves for you, if you are not prepared to carry the same burden for them?

When we have come out into the open, we can see things in a perspective not appreciated before, that if the work that needs to be done in correcting the balance of public opinion regards the truths about our beliefs. This is difficult but not impossible, the more people doing it, the more people that get to know about our ways. THE MATTHEW HOPKINS FILE gives you sound advice on how to combat the bigotry & hysteria that is now generating about Paganism, available from the address at the front of this book.

Being a Pagan who is not afraid of explaining their beliefs, really is a warrior path, & for that you have to be open, after all, whoever heard of a warrior that hid?

INTERESTED IN MAGICK & WITCHCRAFT ?
SUBSCRIBE TO DEOSIL DANCE TODAY!

THE DEOSIL DANCE
The Journal of Pagan beliefs today

ISSUE 33

SAMHAIN 1992

THE DEOSIL DANCE is a quarterly journal that has been regularly published to promote the old ways It is considered by the Occult community to be thought provoking, revolutionary, controversial, this has to be down to the way in which controversial issues are put forward by a myriad of well known contributors & authors. In a well balanced way, there is much for both the beginner, the adept, the curious & the committed

Published 4 times a year on the Greater Sabbats, it is produced in an extremely high quality glossy hard cover A5 format with a least 44 pages in each issue, which, is amazing value for just £8.00 per year. The advantages for subscribers are immense, not only do you get advance notice of new products etc, but you also get advance notification of unique special offers. As well as a high quality magazine 4 times per year, all subscribers are regularly offered free gifts, special offers, special purchases, plus

SUBSCRIBERS ALSO GET A 10% DISCOUNT OFF ALL FUTURE PURCHASES WITH PENTACLE ENTERPRISES.